Centers Made Simple

Centers Made Simple

A Management and Activity Guide

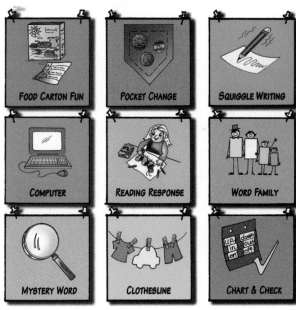

FOOD CARTON FUN   POCKET CHANGE   SQUIGGLE WRITING

COMPUTER   READING RESPONSE   WORD FAMILY

MYSTERY WORD   CLOTHESLINE   CHART & CHECK

by Laureen Reynolds

Crystal Springs
BOOKS
A division of SDE Staff Development for EDUCATORS

Peterborough, New Hampshire

Published by Crystal Springs Books

A division of Staff Development for Educators (SDE)

10 Sharon Road, PO Box 500

Peterborough, NH 03458

1-800-321-0401

www.crystalsprings.com

www.sde.com

Published 2005

Printed in the United States of America

09 08 07 06 05   1 2 3 4 5

ISBN-13: 978-1-884548-78-9

ISBN-10: 1-884548-78-4

Library of Congress Cataloging-in-Publication Data

Reynolds, Laureen, 1969-
  Centers made simple : a management and activity guide / by Laureen Reynolds.
        p. cm.
  Includes bibliographical references.
  ISBN 1-884548-78-4
  1. Classroom learning centers—United States—Planning. 2. Education, Primary—
Activity programs—United States. I. Title.
        LB3044.82.R49 2005
        372.13'3—dc22

Editor: Sandra J. Taylor

Art Director, Designer, and Production Coordinator: Soosen Dunholter

Illustrator: Joyce Orchard Garamella

CONTENTS

INTRODUCTION

Centers *can be* simple and easy to manage. But just the thought of using centers drives fear into some educators' hearts. How will I manage them? What materials should I use? How will everyone know what to do and where to go? How will I manage the paperwork? I had those same questions and watched a colleague in awe for several years before taking the plunge myself. Five years later, I am still employing and enjoying centers with my second-grade class. They are an integral and important part of each day for my students and for me. They allow us to move, share, learn, create, explore materials, and stretch our brains. Our centers time flexes with us and with our sometimes-hectic schedules, and it can be adjusted to meet our needs.

Centers are a vehicle by which you can gain additional one-on-one and small group teaching time. While students are busy with centers, you can call small reading groups together or give individual attention to struggling learners. Centers also give breathing room to your curriculum because many projects can be done simultaneously. They build independence in your students because each child is responsible for completing a certain amount of work in a certain amount of time. Centers provide a venue for reviewing skills and topics efficiently because at each center a child is engaged in a different skill or subject area previously taught. Centers even squeeze in a little bit of fun by giving children opportunities to use a variety of novel materials like highlighters, bean bag chairs, and pocket charts and by allowing time for art projects that might otherwise be cut out of a busy day.

Because centers naturally incorporate movement and choice, they also allow you to address many learning styles and work preferences. They offer your students opportunities to work in ways that are best suited to them each day. Centers are valuable to all students—special education right on through to the gifted and talented. Centers build time into your day for anecdotal notes and informal assessments by creating a window of opportunity for you to walk the room and monitor progress and understanding, and they readily provide home-school connections because parents see each week's worth of center products and learn just what is being taught.

Once you start, you will be able to envision ways to create centers using many objects and locations you already have in your classroom, such as filing cabinets, desks, and doors. Once you start, your colleagues will want to know your secrets and methods for making centers work so well. Once you start, you won't know what you did without them.

MANAGEMENT GUIDELINES

The techniques suggested on the following pages are the product of trial and error, of nipping and tucking, and polishing and trimming my own centers' routines. Remember that these are guidelines, not hard-and-fast rules that must be followed word-by-word. Every classroom is unique. Your students, your physical space, your teaching style, and your curriculum will all influence the centers you choose and how they are used.

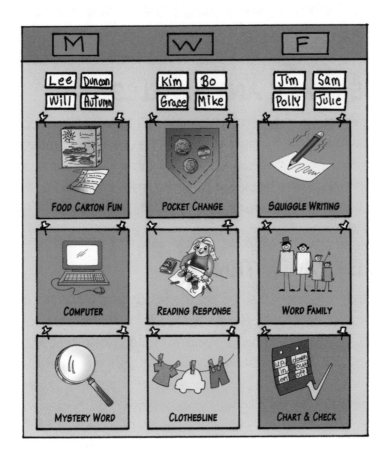

Getting Started

SET A TIME FRAME

Determine how much time can be devoted to centers each day or week. Establishing a time frame will help you figure out how many centers to put on the schedule. If one-hour sessions are possible, children may be able to complete four or five centers during that period. If less time is available, schedule fewer centers. Adjustments to expectations can also be made mid-stream, as well. You will develop a realistic sense for your students' capabilities after a week or two.

REINFORCE THE SKILLS

Examine your curriculum for skills that can be reinforced at center time. For example, reading programs currently used by your school or district may have specific vocabulary or spelling words that could be incorporated into the Word Hunt, Make-a-Word, or Computer centers. Math concepts like patterning, skip counting, number sequencing, or addition and subtraction facts can be reinforced at the Clothesline, Smiley Face, or Play It centers. Such skills are the seeds of great centers.

BE FRANK AND FEARLESS

Explain to your students that you are all learning about centers together. Let them know that some things may need to be changed or moved once the center adventure gets started and that their input is important. Using the management guidelines in this book will eliminate many of the bumps for you, but each space and community of students will have its own needs.

BE CONSISTENT

You already know that the key to encouraging a child's best performance is consistency. When children are familiar with the basic routines, their brains can focus on the skill at hand. Keeping centers consistent will also save you time and energy, as you will not have to keep reminding your students what to do or how to do it. For example, each week at the Word Hunt center, children know they will be locating and highlighting vocabulary words. The words change each week, but the method for completing the center does not.

Explaining the Concept

SAY IT, SIGN IT

Establishing a picture or symbol to go with each center is a quick and easy way to help students locate and identify centers. Ready-to-use symbols for the centers mentioned in this book are provided on pages 51–73, and includes a duplicate set for your schedule board (see page 15). Or you may prefer to make your own. When introducing a center (see page 12), start by explaining the symbol and center name you have decided on. Both of these should reflect what is being used or accomplished at the center. For example, a center where students are required to use clothespins and a clothesline could simply be called Clothesline. A drawing of a clothesline might be an appropriate symbol to use because it is easily recognizable to children. You will need two of each symbol: one will be placed on the schedule board and one will be placed at the center site.

INTRODUCE THE CENTERS

After you reveal the symbol and the name, have the whole group follow you to the center location. Model your expectations for materials use, center maintenance, and final products. Then, give each child an opportunity to experience the center first hand.

Introduce only one center at a time, and do not try to get through all of them in one day. This would be too much information for your students to handle. Try exploring two or three centers a day with second and third graders but just one new center each day with first graders and/or struggling learners.

EXPLAIN PORTABLE CENTERS

Each center does not need its own workspace. Although some, like an Art center, lend themselves to having a specific area, others, such as Make-a-Word or Squiggle Writing, can be taken to a desk or a table, placed on a clipboard or lap desk, or used on the floor or on a rug. A basket or bucket to hold materials and a location on a bookshelf or table is all that is required. This helps tremendously with the space limitations that most teachers have.

STEPS FOR INTRODUCING CENTERS

1. Show students the picture or symbol that goes with the center.

2. Tell them the name of the center.

3. Guide them to the center, whether it is stationary like the Art center or portable like Make-a-Word.

4. Explain the process: If it is Clothesline, show children how to manipulate the clothespins,

how to open and close the container they are stored in, and how to clip the clothespin and the paper shape onto the line. Next, model how to take the paper shape and clothespin off the line and return them to their appropriate storage containers.

5. Give each child a clothespin and a paper shape and let him practice putting them on and taking them off the line.

6. If a center requires the children to record their answers, show them where to find the papers and pencils they will use. With younger children, be sure to model handwriting and spacing expectations.

7. Show children how the center should look when they leave so it is ready for the next person. This may require mixing up word cards so they are not in order, carefully breaking up puzzle pieces, or taking sentence strips out of the pocket chart and placing them at the bottom of the chart so the next student can re-order them.

PRACTICE, PRACTICE, PRACTICE

Provide students with time to practice under your guidance before expecting them to use a center on their own. Some centers, like Word Family, Squiggle Writing, or Book Study, may be practiced as a whole group because they contain a paper for each student. Others, such as Computer, Chart & Check, or Clothesline, may require children to take turns individually because there is only one set of materials to use. It is important to watch your students closely as they practice each center and to reiterate your expectations about the use of materials, the quality of the center's product, and the children's behavior. Having them practice during independent work times, like quiet reading, will allow the others to be busy while you are guiding a few at a time in a particular center.

MODEL THE MATERIALS

It is important to practice with the actual materials as well. Model how you want these tools to be used and put away, and then let the children experience and use them. Modeling is a powerful tool and may be necessary with everything from glue sticks to computers. During the first few weeks of center sessions (and sometimes even later than that!), you may find a center that has not been taken care of according to your specifications. In this situation it is important to let the children be the detectives and figure out what needs to be done. It may

be as simple as pushing in chairs or putting puzzle pieces back into their correct box, but observing it and fixing it together will reinforce your expectations. The children are responsible for the materials, so if something is askew, let them handle it.

CREATE CHILD-FRIENDLY HOMES FOR MATERIALS

After modeling the materials, consider their accessibility to the students. Children will be able to maneuver independently through a center's session if everything they need is at their fingertips. This may mean moving low bookshelves near the art and writing centers for storing art supplies, highlighters, pencils, and erasers. Place containers there too, like wire baskets for papers, dish pans for poetry books, and small plastic, divided carryalls with handles for centers with a lot of pieces, like Make-a-Word. Inexpensive plastic shoeboxes are another great storage tool. They come in different sizes and do not take up much space. Extra student desks can also provide a great work or storage space for the Books on Tape or Smiley Face centers.

PROVIDE EXTRAS

One of the many benefits of centers is that they allow children to choose, move, and learn. Giving children a variety of working spaces and materials will enhance the experience, decrease behavior issues, and increase productivity. Clipboards, lap desks, quiet niches with one or two desks, and bean bag chairs make portable centers appealing. Multicolored highlighters, rubber stamps, and magnets provide extra incentive at stationary centers. Other "extras" to consider are colored pencils, small wipe-off boards and markers, and smiley face stickers.

Making It Work

GET TO WORK

Once centers have been developed, introduced, and stocked with materials, it's time to get started. The tried-and-true methods described here for using centers will get you headed in the right direction. You will quickly discover what works and what does not. Do not be afraid to change things once your children have traveled through a session or two. Sometimes small adjustments like rearranging supplies or moving a group of desks slightly will make a big difference in the general flow of center time.

SET UP A SCHEDULE

Decide where you want to set up the schedule. The place you choose should be easily visible to your students from anywhere in your room and should readily accept thumbtacks, tape, magnets, or staples, so that the process of attaching and rearranging the center symbols and nametags is quick and easy. Any cork, bulletin, or white board will do, as long as it's approximately 3 feet by 3 feet. Write each child's name on a piece of oak tag and laminate it for durability. If you're lucky enough to have a magnetic chalk or white board, attach magnetic tape (which can be found in any craft store) to the back of the children's nametags and the center symbols. (See pages 51–73 for ready-to-use materials.)

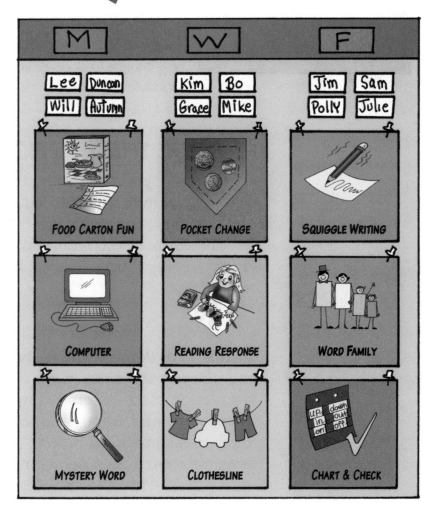

M	W	F
Lee Duncan Will Autumn	Kim Bo Grace Mike	Jim Sam Polly Julie
FOOD CARTON FUN	POCKET CHANGE	SQUIGGLE WRITING
COMPUTER	READING RESPONSE	WORD FAMILY
MYSTERY WORD	CLOTHESLINE	CHART & CHECK

PICK THE TIME FRAME

The number of days you choose to do centers each week depends on your individual schedule. If you plan on five days a week, divide student nametags into five groups and pin each group horizontally across the board. These are not traditional groups (the students will not all work together on a center), and they can change at any time. The purpose of grouping names is simply to split up the traffic going to any one center. Under each group of names, place the pictures of the centers you want those students to complete during that session. The number of symbols you use depends on the time frame you have decided on.

SELECT DAILY CENTERS

After the children find their names at the top of a column, they are free to choose any center symbol in that column to work on. Once they've completed a center, they refer back to their schedule and decide where to go next. Children are responsible for completing all the centers on their schedule each day. The next day their names will be moved over one column, and they will have three or more new centers to do that day. Each symbol appears only once on the schedule for the week.

MANAGE THE TRAFFIC FLOW

To avoid a traffic jam at a stationary center, use chairs to determine how many children can be there at once. For instance, at the Art center, if you want only three children working there at a time, provide only three chairs. When all three are occupied, the other children who have art that day will have to move on to something else until there is a vacant seat. Once children know this rule, it works out quite well.

Quick Tip: Some children have difficulty moving from one place to the next in an efficient manner or without distracting others. Some simply have trouble organizing themselves and waste a lot of time trying to do so. Show these students how to get all of the materials they need for their scheduled centers at the beginning of the session. This will reduce distractions and increase productivity of the group.

OFFER CHOICES

Make specific "choices" available to children who finish their centers before the end of the session so they do not distract others who are still working. Some ideas for choices are puzzles, hidden pictures, computer programs, a selected group of books that relate to some unit you are working on, and ready-made games from companies like The Mailbox, Evan-Moor, Teaching and Learning Company, Crystal Springs Books, and other educational publishers (see Resources, page 50). These games are colorful, easy to use, and usually reinforce phonics, reading, and math skills. You may want to laminate game pieces for durability. Choices can also include working with things like magnetic letters and a cookie sheet or pattern blocks and tracers—anything that will keep children engaged and interested.

Quick Tip: If a student is having trouble managing her time, give her a kitchen timer—an easy and effective tool to use. Most children move themselves right on through the centers, however, because of the option of doing a "choice" when they finish all of them.

Evaluating Progress

WATCH AND WAIT

For the first week, it is important to watch your students work through center sessions and to make note of any trouble spots. See if children have difficulty accessing materials or if a center does not have enough room for them to work properly. Make note of times that the children come to you for help and see if any of those situations can be changed. For instance, if children are seeking you out because they cannot turn on the tape player or cannot reach the top of the pocket chart, then address those issues accordingly. No matter how well you plan, there will always be the need for a few minor adjustments. The time spent doing this will ensure easier and more productive sessions in the future.

WHERE DO ALL THE PAPERS GO?

Although not all centers will yield a tangible product, it is important for students to know what to do with their finished work. Assign each student a special folder for the papers produced from the center sessions that week. At the end of the week, collect the folders for review. Packets of papers can be sent home the following Monday with corrections and, if necessary, requests for student completion of unfinished work. This serves as a natural home-school connection as well. The papers will allow parents to see what concepts are being taught and what skills may require additional review.

Quick Tip: Make the folders all the same color so the children can easily distinguish their centers folders from the others in their desks. It is also helpful to write each child's name on the folder so misplaced ones can be returned easily. When collecting them, you can simply ask for their yellow (or whatever color) folders.

TROUBLESHOOT QUESTIONS

Children will automatically want to come to you when they need help with directions or locating a center or materials. Since, eventually, you may be involved in small-group work or one-on-one check-ins during center sessions, teach students the phrase, "Ask three, then me." Explain that this means they should ask three friends for assistance before seeking you out. Chances are one of the three friends will know the answer, thus preserving your individual teaching time.

Quick Tip: If students finish their centers early, encourage them to check their centers folders for incomplete work and for any papers that could use some attention regarding handwriting, effort, or quality. A few centers, like Puzzles, will not have a paper product. In this case, a child should seek out a peer, a classroom aide, a parent volunteer, or you to check her product before taking it apart.

CENTERS & ACTIVITIES

As you begin your exciting journey into the world of centers, remember that they are intended to provide students with regular opportunities to review, reinforce, and practice skills and concepts previously taught by you. The activities children are asked to complete each week should not be chosen randomly just to fill time. Paying close attention to academic areas will keep centers meaningful for you and your students. The centers and activities I've included here will get you started, but soon you will be developing your own versions. Feel free to change the names of the centers to whatever would be most appropriate for your grade level and teaching style.

Word Work

CLOTHESLINE

Tape or tie a 3- to 5-foot piece of thin rope between two table legs. Provide a small container full of wooden spring-type clothespins. Children clip paper shapes to the line in an order determined by you.

- ◉ For letter identification, write each uppercase letter on small T-shirts made out of construction paper and write each lowercase letter on small pairs of shorts, also made out of construction paper (see reproducibles on pages 75–76). The children are responsible for clipping the uppercase and lowercase versions of each letter together on the clothesline.

- ◉ Using the same pieces mentioned above, have children clip the letters (either uppercase or lowercase) on the line in alphabetical order.

- ◉ Write sight words or spelling words on paper shapes or index cards and have children clip the words on the line in alphabetical order and then record them on paper so their work can be checked. If you have volunteers in the room, they can check the answers right on the line, so recording would not be necessary.

- ◉ Write short phrases retelling a familiar story on paper shapes or index cards and have children clip them to the line in the sequence in which they happened. This is a great comprehension builder!

- ◉ Laminate story pictures drawn by you or the children and have students clip the pictures to the line in the order in which they happened in the story.

- ◉ Write each word of a sentence on paper shapes, index cards, or sentence strip pieces and mix them up. Children read the words and clip them to the line in an order that makes a complete sentence.

PLAY IT

This center may vary from week to week if you use games you already own, but here are a couple of suggestions. Provide lined paper appropriate for your grade level and the assembled dice cutouts on pages 77–81. (Or use a pair of large dice made from blocks of wood, foam, or other suitable material.) Be sure that each die is a different color, so that children know to always put the green one, for example, first because it contains the initial consonant or blend.

- ⊙ On one die write initial consonants or blends like "s," "t," "m," "r," "dr," and "fl." On the other die write short vowel word families like "at," "ot," "ip," "ug," "an," and "et." Children roll the dice and try to produce words. They record the words they made to show their work.

- ⊙ Use the idea mentioned above but write long vowel families like "ake," "ote," "ule," "ice," "ane," and "eat" on one die.

MAKE-A-WORD

Supply this center with the letter and word tiles provided on pages 83–89, plus a laminated sentence strip and a dry-erase marker. Or, if you prefer, make color tiles from oak tag with your own sight, spelling, and vocabulary words. Be sure to laminate them for durability.

◉ At this center, a child chooses a word tile and places it on the sentence strip. Then he makes the same word with letter tiles and places them on the strip next to the word. Finally, he writes the word on the sentence strip with the marker. After making and reading the word three times, he can move on to another word.

◉ This center can be used each week by simply changing the words the children are making.

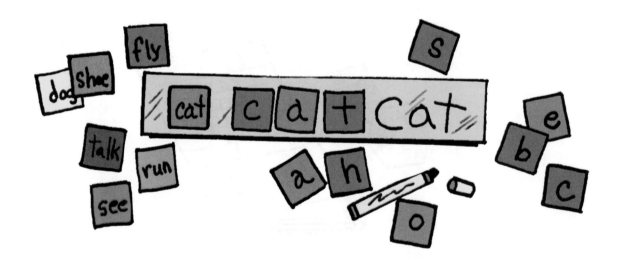

BOOK STUDY

Many reproducible mini-books are available for the educational market. These books often focus on a specific sound, word ending, or letter. The books are often thematic as well, so they might tie in to a unit of study like insects or plants and seeds. Provide children with a mini-book and

highlighters. If you do not own a resource book like this, ask your colleagues, or check the resource section at the back of this book for additional titles that you may find helpful. Many school and public libraries have teacher resource sections as well.

- ◉ Have children highlight a particular letter each time they see it. This is good practice for your youngest students.

- ◉ As children become readers, have them locate and highlight a specific word each time they come across it. This is great for reinforcing sight words.

- ◉ Ask children to highlight a particular word family (like "at") each time it appears in the text.

- ◉ Have them highlight a short or long vowel sound, pre-determined by you, as they see it in the story.

- ◉ For older children, consider checking out Evan-Moor's **Read and Understand** series. The passages in these books not only provide valuable reading practice at appropriate levels but also are accompanied by comprehension, sequencing, and phonics activities.

Centers & Activities

SMILEY FACE

Provide an assortment of small smiley face stickers. Each week, when visiting this center, the children will be required to determine if something is right or wrong and place the smiley faces on top of correct items.

- ◉ Type sentences but purposefully omit some necessary uppercase letters. Children will need to place a smiley face over the letters that should be uppercase (for example, the beginning of a sentence, the date, or a name).

- ◉ Write a contraction next to a pair of words. If the words when combined make the contraction, children place a smiley face over them. For example, **do not = don't** would receive a smiley face.

- ◉ Provide a paper with pairs of words, some that are antonyms (opposites), like "on and off," and some that are not, like "up and in." Children place a smiley face sticker over the pairs that are true opposites. Extend the activity to include synonyms and homonyms as well.

- ◉ Supply this center with a list of familiar words or your spelling words for the week. If the word is spelled correctly, it gets a smiley face. If it is not, the student spells it correctly on the paper.

- ◉ Use a combination of correct and incorrect punctuation in a group of sentences you have typed. Be sure to include a variety of examples (questions, exclamations, and statements). Children stick a smiley face next to the sentences that contain the correct punctuation. If you wish, ask them also to fix the ones that are punctuated incorrectly.

Quick Tip: If you do not have access to stickers, provide special colored pens so the students can simply draw smiley faces instead.

SORTING SACK

Fill a small sack or bag with two sets of word or picture cards and have children sort the cards into two categories. There should be the same number of one category as of another, so if you have four *long o* words, you should also include four *short o* words. Provide a sheet of paper with two columns of lines. At the top of each column, place a category name (*long o* and *short o*, or *spelled right* and *not spelled right*, for example). Children are responsible for sorting the cards into two piles and recording their answers in the appropriate column on their paper.

- ◉ short-vowel and long-vowel words (see pages 99–101)
- ◉ correctly spelled and incorrectly spelled words (see pages 103–105)
- ◉ hard things and soft things
- ◉ animals and people
- ◉ summer activities and winter activities
- ◉ one-, two-, and (if your students are already good readers) three-syllable words (see pages 105–107). Have children sort words into piles according to the number of syllables they contain. If you include three-syllable words, add another column to the paper children will use for recording their answers.

Quick Tip: For younger children or those who have trouble with paper and pencil tasks, make a set of cards for each child and let him glue the cards in the correct column. This offers an additional benefit of developing fine motor skills.

WORD FAMILY

A variety of teacher resource books (see Resources, page 50) are available that are filled with word family activities, such as Scholastic's **Fun Phonics Manipulatives** and **Word Family Tales**. These books provide reproducibles you may want to use in a center. You probably already have word family activities you use regularly that may work as well. Here are some additional suggestions.

⦿ Create a flip-book using the word family you want to focus on. Cut a sheet of 8½-by-11-inch paper in half horizontally. Divide one of the halves in half by drawing a vertical black line. Write the word family on the right side of the line. On the left side, staple a stack of three to five smaller squares of blank paper. Ask the children to write an initial letter or a blend on the blank squares to make rhyming words. So, if the word family is "ine," the children might write "n" on a square to make "nine," "m" on another square to make "mine," and so on.

⦿ Divide a sheet of paper into 6 equal squares, leaving room at the top for the child's name and the title "Word Family" (see sample, right). At the bottom of each square write a word in the word family you are teaching. Children are responsible for reading the word and creating an illustration for each word.

⦿ Using the same format mentioned above, leave a blank space or two in front of the word family, let the children make their own word and then illustrate it. More advanced children may also enjoy the challenge of trying to use all of the words in a silly sentence.

WORD HUNT

Each week use your vocabulary or spelling words in this center. If you do not have specific word lists you are required to teach, use five or six sight words or words that are pertinent to the science or social studies unit you are currently studying.

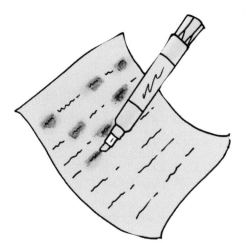

◉ Type the words in big print at the top of a sheet of paper and then incorporate them into sentences on the rest of the page, using each word in more than one sentence. Children visiting this center will use a highlighter to color the vocabulary words each time they appear on the page. (Children who have trouble tracking or recognizing words can cut out the word at the top of the page and move it underneath each sentence as they read. This will help them find a word that matches without having to look back up at the top of the page.)

◉ On index cards or a matrix, write the vocabulary words you wish to focus on. Each time a child finds that word in a book he is reading, he can make a check mark on the index card or inside the box.

◉ Incorporate the week's words into a word search. You can make your own word search using graph paper, or check the Internet for free downloads and make a new one each week. Children highlight the words as they find them. Word searches improve visual tracking—an essential skill for successful reading.

MYSTERY WORD

Scramble the letters in a word and ask the children to figure out what the word is. Practice first with simple words consisting of only a few letters until the children are comfortable with the process.

◉ Use a different child's name each time you do Mystery Word in the beginning of the year. This will provide great practice for learning how to spell classmate's names, and your students will love to see their names as the focus of an activity.

◉ Choose a calendar term or a math vocabulary word. Select the letter tiles from pages 83–85 that spell the word and place those tiles in a small container. Children can take the container to their desks, remove the tiles, and spell different words by moving the tiles around and by adding or deleting tiles when necessary.

◉ Choose a long word that is related to your story for the week or to a science or social studies unit. Using the reproducible on page 109, scramble the letters and write them at the top of the page. In the boxes below, children write words using the scrambled letters. If the word you selected is, for example, **airplane,** you would scramble the letters, which might look like **ralenipa,** and write them at the top of the page. Children may find words like **plan**, **line**, **rail**, and **are**, along with many others. Encourage them to try to figure out what the mystery word is and to write it down as well. They will love the challenge of the mystery and come up with some great words in the meantime.

Mystery Word

NAME : _____

Use these letters to make words and write them in the boxes below. ralenipa

ran	are	line	pea
pan	ripe	plan	ape

Can you figure out the Mystery Word? _____

COMPUTER

Choose one child from the group each day to start and the rest can flow through the center as it becomes available. Providing kitchen timers and a time limit of 10 minutes will keep children from staying there too long. It is important to model any programs that your students will eventually use independently. A painting and drawing program like Kid Pix is a wonderful, child-friendly way to integrate technology into your center routine. Kid Pix offers a large picture library and many tools for students to create original art pieces.

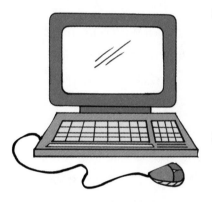

- ◉ Children type spelling or vocabulary words. This is a novel way for students to review important words, and it also strengthens their keyboard knowledge and typing skills. Be sure your students print out their work and place it in their centers folders so it can be checked at the end of the week.

- ◉ Using painting and drawing software, students make and fill in a six-cell matrix by "stamping" rhyming words or words that begin with the same letter in each box. You can also prepare a matrix with pictures already in each box for your students to label when they arrive at the computer.

- ◉ Children "stamp" pictures from a drawing and painting program like Kid Pix and label each one using the keyboard or virtual letter stamps. Ask them to choose pictures that represent a letter sound or word family you are working on. For example, if the letter for the week is "Mm," then children can stamp pictures that begin with that sound, like man, mirror, map, etc. Or, if "at" is the word family you are focusing on, children can stamp and label pictures of a cat, mat, hat, etc.

- ◉ Students hunt through a program's picture library for pictures of things that have a certain vowel sound and stamp them onto the screen. If the program has a large picture library, you may want to direct your students to use only certain sections of the library to save time. Preview each section so you can make recommendations. If, for example, your students are looking for sea animal pictures, you could tell them to start with the "Nature" and "Outdoors" picture libraries.

FOOD CARTON FUN

Supply this center with clean, empty food containers like cereal boxes, coffee cans, and milk cartons. Inside each one, place a skill card that directs the child to do a certain task with the container. The cards can be changed each week in order to focus on particular skills.

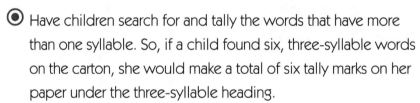

◉ Ask children to find all the words on the container that begin with a certain letter and write down the total number.

◉ Have students record a specific number of words from the container that describe the product that used to be inside. For example, a cereal box may have words like "crunchy," "nutty," or "sweet."

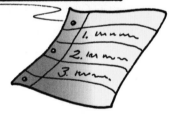

◉ Have children search for and tally the words that have more than one syllable. So, if a child found six, three-syllable words on the carton, she would make a total of six tally marks on her paper under the three-syllable heading.

◉ Ask students to find words that have a silent-, long-, or short-vowel sound.

◉ Have children count the number of words on the front of the container.

Writing

HANDWRITING

Many school districts have handwriting practice pages that are required for children in the primary grades. Handwriting does not have to be limited to pre-made pages, but it helps with time management of crowded curriculums.

- After demonstrating the formation of each letter and practicing it as a group, include a practice page at the center for children to review how to write this letter. Each week you can feature a different letter.

- For younger children, provide a 4-by-6-inch index card for each child with the letter of the week written on it so that it covers most of the card. Place a green circle sticker at the starting point for making the letter and an arrow showing the direction in which the pencil would travel when making the letter. Also, provide sheets of circle stickers of other colors. Children should cover the letter you wrote with stickers, following the lines you made when writing the letter. Then they should trace over it with their fingers a number of times. They can say the sound of the letter, too, while tracing it with their fingers. Punch a hole in the corner of each card so children can build a ring of tactile letters to remind them how to form each one. Provide chicken rings, binder rings, brads, or some other material to hold the cards together.

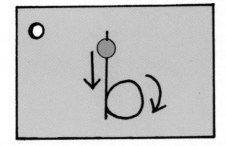

Centers & Activities

SQUIGGLE WRITING

This center will attract both artists and writers. It allows for creativity and individuality while offering fine motor skill practice for all.

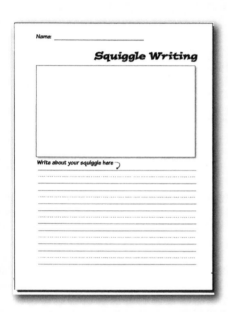

- Use the reproducible on page 110. In the box, make a squiggle mark with a dark pen before you copy it for everyone. The mark can be a zigzag, a half circle, a swirl, or anything at all. The children are responsible for creating a picture from the squiggle and writing creatively about it on the lines below.

- Each week, let a different child make the squiggle, and repeat the process above. At the end of the week, collect all the squiggle papers, staple them together, and give them to the child who created the original squiggle.

- Make a different squiggle on 12 index cards and put the cards in a small bag. Have the child pull a card from the bag, reproduce the squiggle by hand on his paper, and repeat the process above. Children enjoy the grab-bag aspect of this activity.

JOURNAL WRITING

Create a journal for each student, using two pieces of 9-by-12-inch construction paper as the front and back covers and stapling any number of lined pieces of paper in between. Also provide a writing prompt

each week. Prompts can be something simple, like "Describe your last birthday," or more complicated, such as "Would you have liked being one of the original Pilgrims? Tell me why or why not." Obviously, the topic would need to be appropriate for the age and abilities of your students.

- Review teachers' magazines for writing prompts. Many, like **The Mailbox**, offer a month full of writing prompts all on one page. Thematic and monthly teacher resource books do as well.

- Brainstorm topics with your students and use one idea each week.

- Place a dozen or so topics, written on index cards, inside a pail or a box and have students draw out cards when it is their time to write. This way you will receive journal entries on a variety of topics each week.

- Give your young writers a specific task each week, like writing a grocery list, an invitation to a party, a children's menu, or a recipe. Be sure to provide real life samples of the items so children can learn about the vocabulary and format of each.

Reading

CHART & CHECK

This center is helpful in reinforcing both reading skills and weekly vocabulary words. It offers children a chance to use materials like pocket charts and sentence strips, and it can even boost their fluency because they are re-reading sentences, lines to a poem, or story parts.

◉ Each week place four to six sentence strips in a pocket chart with a blank space where a vocabulary word would make sense. Write each vocabulary word on an index card and place the pile of cards at the top of the pocket chart. Children are responsible for reading the sentences and deciding which word fits in each sentence. Once all the blanks are filled in, each child must read the sentences to another student to check for accuracy.

◉ To make this more challenging, write each sentence on a different color sentence strip, cut the strip into pieces, and place them in the pocket chart in an order that does not make sense. The children are then responsible for putting the sentences in the correct order and reading them to a classmate.

◉ Use the lines of a familiar poem with the idea above; a poem that rhymes will be the best choice for most young students.

◉ In each pocket of the chart, place a piece of paper of a different color. At the top of the chart, supply index cards with the names of the corresponding colors written on them. Students need to match the word for the name of the color to the appropriately colored piece of paper.

⦿ Place simple pictures in the pockets of the chart and provide the corresponding words on cards at the top of the chart. Children match the words at the top to the pictures already in the chart. (See ready-to-use materials on pages 111-117.)

⦿ Fill the pockets with words that have an obvious opposite partner (for example, **on/off**, **in/out**, and **hot/cold**) and have children match up the antonym pairs. The same activity also can be used with synonyms. (See ready-to-use materials on pages 119-121.)

⦿ Fill the chart with numeral and number word cards that are appropriate for your students. Children need to match the numeral to its correct word. (See ready-to-use materials on pages 123-125.)

⦿ Write the important events of a familiar story, each on a separate sentence strip. Students will need to order the events in the pocket chart. This is a terrific comprehension exercise and provides a good model for students when they do a retelling of their own.

Quick Tip: For durability, be sure to laminate the ready-to-use materials provided in this book, as well as any other pieces that will be handled frequently at your centers. Store them in a folder, box, or bin, where they will be readily available for another center session.

READING RESPONSE

A large variety of reading response forms will be appropriate for this center. Many of these forms can be quickly and easily made by you, an aide, or a volunteer. Here are some activities to get you started.

- Ask students to choose a character from a book and create a Character Snapshot using a copy of the reproducible on page 127. Students write detailed information about the character, such as his/her likes and dislikes, events that happened to the character, how the character is the same as or different from the student—whatever you choose. Also, have them draw the character in the space provided on the sheet.

- Using a copy of the reproducible on page 128, children create a Story Flag about a story they have read or that you have read to them. They write a few sentences about the story around the inside edge of the flag and create a drawing in the middle of the flag that represents a part of the story.

  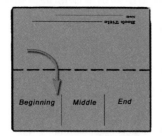

  - Fold a piece of 9-by-12-inch paper in half lengthwise (hot-dog style). Divide one long side into three sections with a black marker. On the first section write "Beginning," on the second section write "Middle," and on the third section write "End." Make a copy for each child and cut along each line to make a three-flap flip book. After reading an appropriate book, each child writes one sentence about the beginning and draws a picture to go with it under the first flap. Under the second flap, she writes and draws about the middle of the book, and under the third flap, she writes and draws about the end. For older children, make the same type of flip book but label the flaps "Characters," "Setting," and "Plot."

  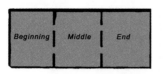

  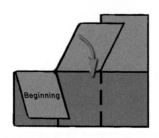

  - For a greater challenge, stack three pages together, make the same type of flip book as described above, and label the top flaps "Beginning," "Middle," and "End." Under the Beginning section, write a different beginning of a story on each of the remaining five flaps; do the same for the Middle and the End sections. Then, the students can make a selection from one of the five flaps under each section and write a story based on what they picked. Each time they go through the book, they can make other selections and have another new story to write.

CLOTHESLINE

This center, which was referenced earlier in the Word Work section, can also work for math. Use the shape patterns on pages 75–76 or create your own.

- ◉ Write the numbers you wish students to sequence on any shapes desired— one number to each shape. Place the shapes in a small container at the clothesline and ask children to pin them up in order. They can record their answers on a worksheet that has the outline of the shape being clipped to the line. This idea works for counting by ones, twos, fives, or tens.

- ◉ Integrate pattern creation and completion into the clothesline. Instead of writing numbers, draw squares, circles, and triangles, for example, and have children create and record three-part patterns.

- ◉ Provide shapes that have a number or a corresponding number of dots on each one. Children clip the number on the line next to the shape containing the correct number of dots.

- ◉ Ask children to clip numbers and their corresponding words to the line in sequence.

- ◉ Select the ready-to-use materials on pages 129-133 that are appropriate for your students, or make your own by stamping sets of coins onto paper shapes or index cards. On another set of cards or shapes, write the money amounts that match the coin sets you stamped. Children clip the coin set next to its corresponding written amount on the clothesline.

SMILEY FACE

This center is similar to the one on page 24 under Word Work. Provide children with smiley face stickers that they will place on a worksheet.

- On a sheet of paper write a number of addition facts with the sums included, but be sure that some of the answers are incorrect. Children figure each equation and place a smiley face over the sums that are correct. If the sum is not correct, the children must supply the correct answer.
- Use the idea above but substitute subtraction for the addition facts.
- Provide a worksheet with sets of coins matched with monetary amounts. Students indicate the correct pairs with stickers.

ESTIMATION

At this center, children are responsible for estimating the number of items in a large, clear jar. They write their guesses and their names on slips of paper and place the papers in a designated spot, like a basket, box, or envelope. At the end of the week, review the slips out loud and reveal the correct answer. As a group, decide whose guess is the closest.

◉ Each week fill a large, clear jar full of small items, such as unifix cubes, macaroni, or small blocks. Have the children guess how many objects are contained in the jar.

◉ Place a chain of paper clips in a clear jar. Tell the children how many clips you used and ask them to estimate how long they think the chain is.

◉ Pose an estimation word problem each week, such as the following: How many unifix cubes do you think will fit in my shoe? How many pennies can we stack before the stack topples over? How much do you think five math books will weigh? At the end of the week, figure out the correct answer and compare it to the children's estimations.

Quick Tip: Instead of repeatedly filling the jar yourself, send it home with a different child each week and have him fill it with something from home, with his parents' permission, of course! Make sure he counts the items he put in and lets you know how many are inside. Then, allow him to be exempt from that center for the week.

COMPUTER

Enhancing your students' computer savvy is always time well spent. Computer-based activities have a high interest level for children, so they are motivated to do their best. This center also gives them a break from paper and pencil tasks.

- Bring math and literacy together at this center by using picture-drawing software like Kid Pix. Most schools own this or something similar, and it is usually available for classroom teachers to borrow. Have the children type a number story or word problem and draw a picture to go with it—all on the computer. A number story might read as follows: "Sally picked 3 flowers from the garden. I picked 2. We gave all of them to Dad. How many flowers does Dad have? Dad has 5 flowers." The child would then draw a picture to go with the story by using the tools provided by the painting and drawing program you are using.

- Have children type fact families on the computer such as $8 + 2 = 10$, $2 + 8 = 10$, $10 - 2 = 8$, $10 - 8 = 2$. They can print out their fact sheets for you to check later. This is great for reinforcing addition and subtraction facts, plus it will strengthen hand muscles, coordination, and typing skills.

- Ask students to type math facts using number words instead of numerals. For example, instead of typing $3 + 4 = 7$, children will type three + four = seven. Young readers and writers can always use a review of number words, and this is a fun way to do just that.

Quick Tip: Check with your math or technology coordinator to see if the manufacturer of your school's math program also produces a CD-ROM of math activities and games children can use on the computer. Many companies do and your school may already possess copies for classroom use.

EGG CARTON COUNTING

Supply this center with a 12-compartment egg carton with a solid lid, 2 bingo chips (each a different color), and a calculator. Each compartment of the egg carton should be labeled with a number from 1 through 12.

- Have the child put the 2 bingo chips in the egg carton, shut the lid, and shake the carton. When he opens the lid, he looks to see where the chips landed and adds together the numbers marked on those compartments. Then he checks his answer with the calculator. To make this more challenging, increase the number of bingo chips.

- Using the same procedure as above, the child does subtraction and multiplication problems based on where the 2 bingo chips landed inside the egg carton.

- Have your students get that all-important math fact practice by making fact families using the two numbers the bingo chips landed on. For example, if the chips landed in the 7 and 3 compartments, the student would write:
  $7 + 3 = 10, 3 + 7 = 10, 10 - 3 = 7, 10 - 7 = 3.$

- Assign a place value to each color of bingo chip. If a red and a green chip are being used, the red could represent the tens place and the green could represent the ones place. After shaking the carton and seeing where the chips landed, the child would write down the number made by adding the tens and ones together. For example, if the red chip landed on the 6, that would be 6 tens, or 60. If the green chip landed on the 2, that would be 2 ones, or 2. The total number for that turn would be 62. To increase the difficulty of this activity, add more bingo chips of different colors to represent other place values.

POCKET CHANGE

On a big piece of foam core or stiff cardboard, draw 9 large pockets. Attach a combination of coins to the front of each pocket with tape or Velcro. The coins can be changed each week and can range in difficulty according to your students' abilities.

- ◉ Using the reproducible on page 135, ask children to record on each pocket the amount of money shown on each large pocket on the big board.
- ◉ Have children figure out how much more money they would need to make $1.00 on each large pocket and record that amount on the reproducible.

MATH SUNS

Make copies of the patterns on page 136 on yellow paper. The circle is for the center of the sun and the five triangles are for its rays. If you wish to reuse the suns week after week, make enough copies so that each child has one, laminate them, and then provide children with wipe-off markers to use.

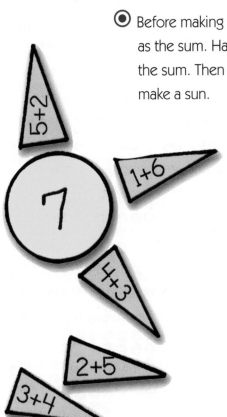

⦿ Before making copies, write a number in the circle. This number will serve as the sum. Have your students write an addition fact in each ray that equals the sum. Then have them cut out all the pieces and glue them together to make a sun.

⦿ Use the idea above to make subtraction suns. The number you write in the circle will represent the difference, so this time your students need to supply equations that equal the difference.

MATH FACTORY

At this center, children use a variety of manipulatives to generate and solve math facts (see ready-to-use materials on pages 137–141).

⦿ Fishing (literally!) is a great way to get students to learn addition and subtraction facts. Laminate and cut out the fish on pages 137–139. Write one math fact on the back of each fish, but do not include the answers, and attach a large paper clip to each one. Make a fishing pole from a wooden dowel with a string tied to it. At the end of the string, hot glue a strong magnet for the hook. This center works best when two children occupy it together. The children place all the fish on the floor in a designated area (the pond) and one of them hooks a fish with the pole. She reads the math fact and figures out the sum or difference. If she is correct, she keeps the fish in her pile; if she is not correct, she throws the fish back and lets the other child have a turn to go fishing.

⦿ Laminate and cut out the chocolate chip cookies on page 141 (or make your own) and place any number of them in a cookie jar, along with some pencils and paper. Be sure your cookies each have a distinct number of chips drawn on them. A child pulls out 2 cookies at a time, counts the chips on each, and writes and solves an addition and a subtraction problem using the number of chips as his guide. For example, if one cookie has six chips on it and the other has two chips on it, he would write: $6 - 2 = 4$ and $6 + 2 = 8$.

⦿ Supply children with dice and a fact-recording sheet. Children roll the dice and use the two numbers rolled to make addition or subtraction facts. To increase the difficulty of this activity, have children use polyhedral dice so they are exposed to larger numbers. Children can also roll three dice to make more complicated addition facts.

SORTING SACK

For this center you will need a small sack or bag. Each week you place items inside it that can be sorted into groups or pairs. You can put real objects inside or index cards showing pictures, numbers, or shapes.

- ⊙ Place any number of buttons inside the sack and have children sort them according to color, size, shape, the number of holes, or other features.

- ⊙ Put attribute blocks inside the sack and ask students to sort them according to thickness, color, shape, or size.

- ⊙ Fill the sack with real or play money (pennies, nickels, dimes, and quarters) and four index cards, each with an amount of money written on it that corresponds to one of the coins inside. Students who are just getting to know their coins can sort out the money according to its worth by placing each coin on the index card that bears its amount. For example, if a child has a penny, he places it on the card that reads "one cent"; if he has a nickel, he places it on the card that reads "five cents."

- ⊙ Place index cards in the sack with numbers written on them that are appropriate for your students' abilities and have children sort them by odd and even or by greater than and less than a number you specify.

- ⊙ For children who are learning to count, have them sort out cards with pictures and corresponding numbers. For example, if a student finds a card with six balloons on it, he looks for the card with the numeral 6 on it. To increase the difficulty, you could add a third card with the number word on it.

Centers & Activities

Arts & Crafts

ART

This center will probably vary from week to week. Be sure to model the use of any new materials as necessary.

- ◉ Cover a table with plastic place mats or a vinyl cloth. Provide an assortment of modeling clay and have the children create letters, numbers, words, shapes, or objects from it. Working with clay is beneficial to hand and arm muscles, which will eventually improve a child's handwriting and other fine motor skills. Some children also find it has a calming effect on them.

- ◉ Throughout the year, collect scraps of colored paper and store them in a box on your art shelves. When you have a sufficient amount, challenge students to create pictures by gluing small, torn pieces of the scrap paper together—no scissors, crayons, or markers allowed. Model the procedure first. You might tear black paper for a cat's head, and then tear and glue blue, pink, and white pieces for its eyes, nose, mouth, whiskers, and ears.

- ◉ Allow children to twist and wind pipe cleaners together to create original art. Display the creations on a table or a bookshelf and call it the Art Gallery.

- ◉ Supply children with multicolored bingo markers (available at most drug and superstores) and white construction paper. Allow them to let their creative juices flow and create original pieces of artwork by "pouncing" the bingo marker on the paper. Model the pouncing technique so children won't attempt to "color" with them like they do with traditional markers.

◉ Many things can be made from the cut out of a hand tracing. The following activities are not only fun but also beneficial for improving fine motor skills:

- Glue many hands together in a circle to form a wreath. Add a bow and hang it with string.

- Make a fish by tracing around a closed hand. The thumb can represent a fin on the fish's back or belly. Have students glue it to a piece of colored paper and create an underwater scene with markers.

- Make a bird from two hands. With palms together, glue the hands along the bottom edge. Have students draw, cut out, and glue on the bird's head.

- Use one hand for the petal part of a tulip and green paper or markers for the stem and leaves.

- Cut out many hands from yellow and orange paper, glue them, with fingers sticking out, to a yellow paper plate to create a sun.

- Create the branches of a tree by cutting a few hands out of brown paper and attaching them to a paper or marker-drawn tree trunk. Have students draw the leaves.

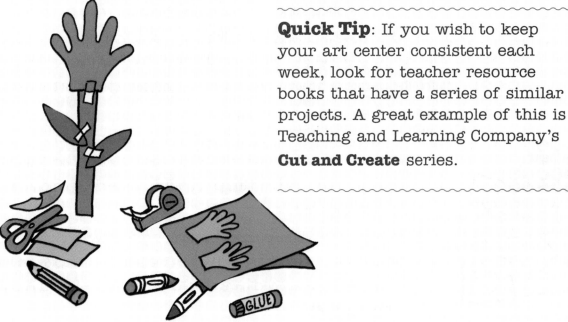

Quick Tip: If you wish to keep your art center consistent each week, look for teacher resource books that have a series of similar projects. A great example of this is Teaching and Learning Company's **Cut and Create** series.

Brain Benders

PUZZLES

Children love puzzles, and putting the pieces together as a group provides an excellent opportunity for them to strengthen teamwork and problem-solving skills. The large variety of puzzles available for the educational market guarantees their appeal to all ages.

⦿ Puzzle centers can be a terrific tie to a theme or unit. If ocean life study is on the schedule for the week, place several ready-made, theme-related puzzles, with varying degrees of difficulty, in the puzzle center. Children can put them together on the floor, at a table, or on their desks.

⦿ Manufactured mazes, hidden pictures, and crossword puzzles for children can be used in this center as well. Scanning your teacher resource books will produce a variety of puzzles, which vary in difficulty. Another good source of puzzles is Evan-Moor's **The Never-Bored Kid** series. **Highlights for Children** magazine also has an annual **Hidden Pictures** book and a series called "Puzzle Mania"; both are full of a variety of enticing brain benders.

⦿ Make your own puzzles by writing words on sheets of oak tag. After laminating each one, cut the sheets apart to create custom-made word puzzles.

⦿ Use the idea above and write an addition or subtraction problem on one half of the oak tag and the solution on the other half. Then cut them apart. Children match the pieces by solving the problems. They can also recite the math facts to a classmate.

⦿ Stamp coins on one half of the oak tag. Write the amount of money represented on the other half and cut each puzzle apart. Students count the coins and find the piece with the matching amount in order to finish each puzzle.

⦿ Make your own time puzzles by stamping or drawing clock faces on one half of the oak tag and writing the time they display on the other half. Cut apart and have children read the clocks and find their matching times.

Listen & Learn

BOOKS ON TAPE

Books on tape make an engaging center for many grade levels. Ready-made tapes can be purchased from book clubs or you can record them yourself. If you make your own, record some stories by "guest readers," such as the school principal, secretary, nurse, or custodian.

- ◉ For younger children, provide a new tape each week, along with a piece of drawing paper with the title of the book written at the top. After listening to the story, children should draw a picture that tells something about the book.

- ◉ For older children, provide a new tape each week as well. Also include a paper that is half blank for a picture and half full of lines for writing. Children should draw a picture and write a few sentences that relate to the story.

Quick Tip: To promote independent use of the tape player, you may need to label the function buttons. Place a green smiley face sticker on the "play" button, a red sticker on the "stop" button, and a yellow sticker on the "rewind" button. The stickers will help children remember the purpose of each button after you have modeled the expected use of the tape player.

Resources

The following list of publications, resource books, and products will further enhance your centers repertoire. These materials are readily available at bookstores, from publisher's catalogs, and on line.

- Teacher magazines like **The Mailbox** and **Teacher's Helper** offer center ideas of all kinds. Your school library may subscribe to one or more of these periodicals, so you can even browse back issues for ideas at any time.

- **Teaching K-8** magazine has ideas for every area of the curriculum. Visit the "Green Pages," included in each issue, for ideas that can be incorporated into your center sessions. For more information, log on to **www.TeachingK-8.com**.

- **Highlights for Children** magazine provides a hidden picture each month (great for the Puzzle Center) and terrific, easy-to-make craft projects that may fit into your Art Center. Go to **www. Highlights.com** to learn more.

- Two great books to get you going on the Word Family Center are Liza Charlesworth's **Turn and Learn Word Family Wheels** (Scholastic, 2000, New York) and Carol Kirkham Martin's **Word Chunks: Activities for Learning Word Families** (Teacher Created Resources, 2003, Westminster, CA). Both books offer countless activity ideas and patterns for hands-on manipulatives for your students.

- If you have your sights set on the Book Study Center, check out **Alpha-Tales** (Teaching Resources, 2004, New York). The set contains a silly reproducible mini-book and a full-color class book for each letter of the alphabet. Deborah Schecter's **My First Little Readers** (Teaching Resources, 2004, New York) is also a wonderful resource full of reproducible books your students can read and highlight.

- The following products, available from Crystal Springs Books (1-800-321-0401; **www. crystalsprings.com**), will add novelty and interest to your centers.

  Language-Building Box: Word and Picture Card Games and Activities by Daphne Byrd and Polly Westfall can be used at Clothesline, Sorting Sack, and Chart & Check for alphabetizing, sorting, sentence building, and more!

  Number Match Games by Donna Whyte shows how the numbers from 1–10 can be represented in many ways by using tally marks, Roman numerals, money, words, dice, etc. This is great for use in Sorting Sack, Clothesline, and Chart & Check.

CLOTHESLINE

PLAY IT

MAKE-A-WORD

BOOK STUDY

WORD WORK

WORD WORK & MATH

WORD WORK

WORD WORK

SMILEY FACE

SORTING SACK

WORD FAMILY

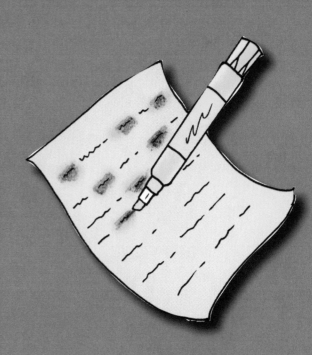

WORD HUNT

WORD WORK & MATH

WORD WORK & MATH

WORD WORK

WORD WORK

MYSTERY WORD

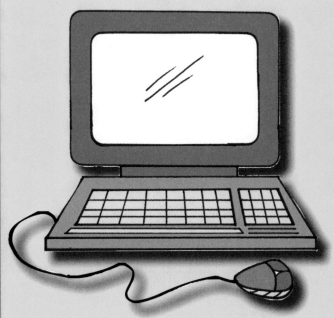

COMPUTER

FOOD CARTON FUN

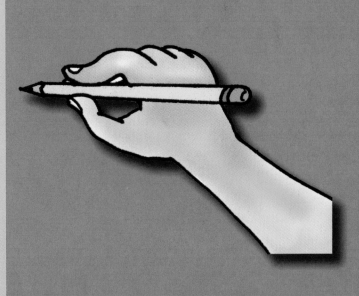

HANDWRITING

WORD WORK & MATH

WORD WORK

WRITING

WORD WORK

SQUIGGLE WRITING

JOURNAL WRITING

CHART & CHECK

READING RESPONSE

WRITING

WRITING

READING

READING

ESTIMATION

EGG CARTON COUNTING

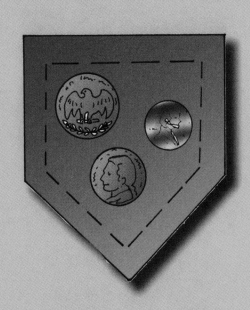

POCKET CHANGE

MATH SUNS

MATH
FACTORY

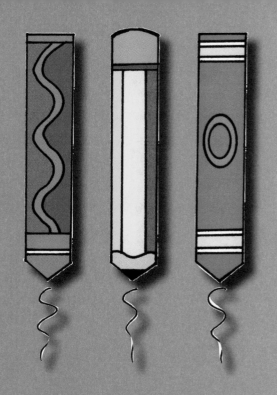

ART

PUZZLES

BOOKS ON TAPE

ART

MATH

LISTEN & LEARN

BRAIN BENDERS

CLOTHESLINE

PLAY IT

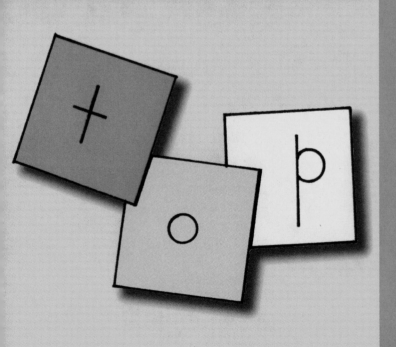

MAKE-A-WORD

BOOK STUDY

WORD WORK

WORD WORK & MATH

WORD WORK

WORD WORK

SMILEY FACE

SORTING SACK

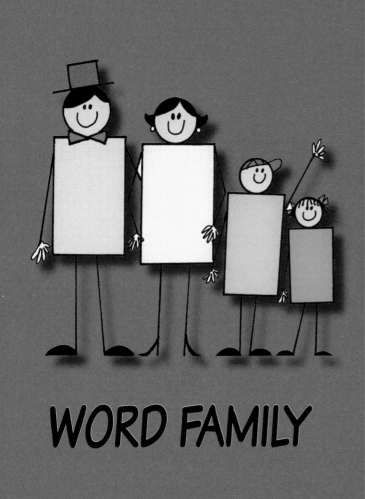

WORD FAMILY

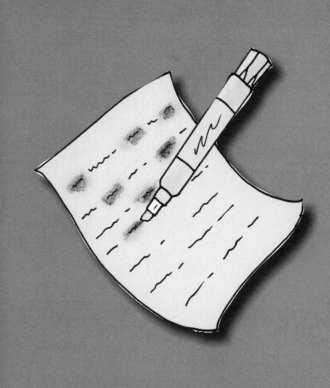

WORD HUNT

WORD WORK & MATH

WORD WORK & MATH

WORD WORK

WORD WORK

MYSTERY
WORD

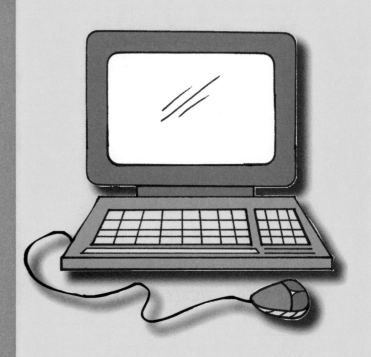

COMPUTER

FOOD CARTON
FUN

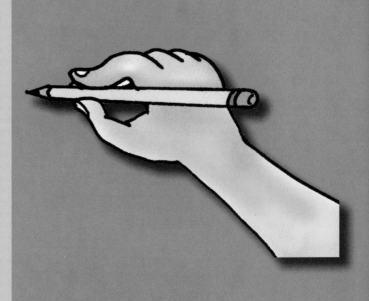

HANDWRITING

WORD WORK & MATH

WORD WORK

WRITING

WORD WORK

SQUIGGLE WRITING

JOURNAL WRITING

CHART & CHECK

READING RESPONSE

WRITING

WRITING

READING

READING

ESTIMATION

EGG CARTON COUNTING

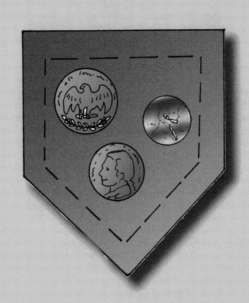

POCKET CHANGE

MATH SUNS

MATH

MATH

MATH

MATH

MATH FACTORY

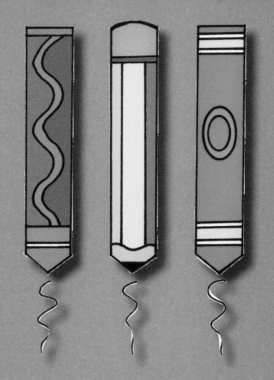

ART

PUZZLES

BOOKS ON TAPE

ART

MATH

LISTEN & LEARN

BRAIN BENDERS

Word Work/ Clothesline–Reproducible

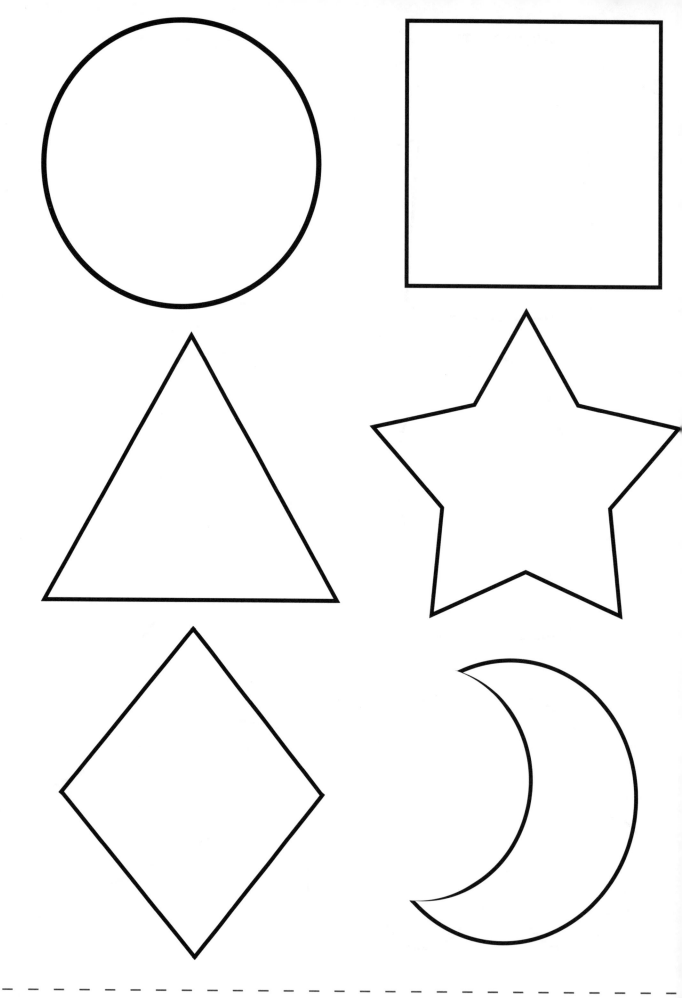

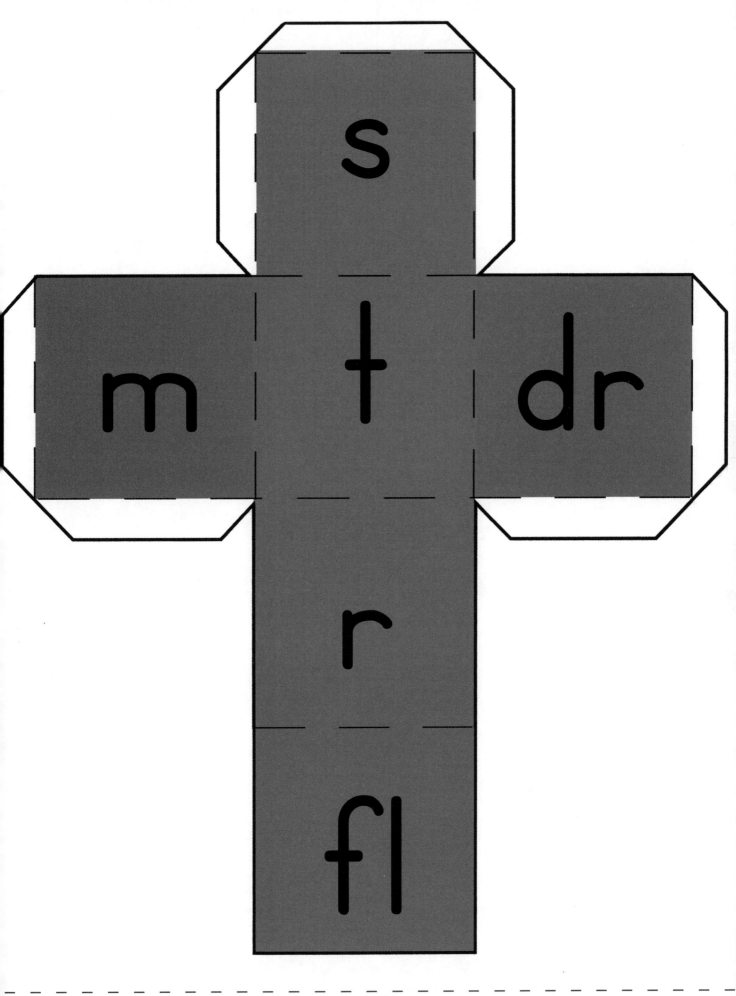

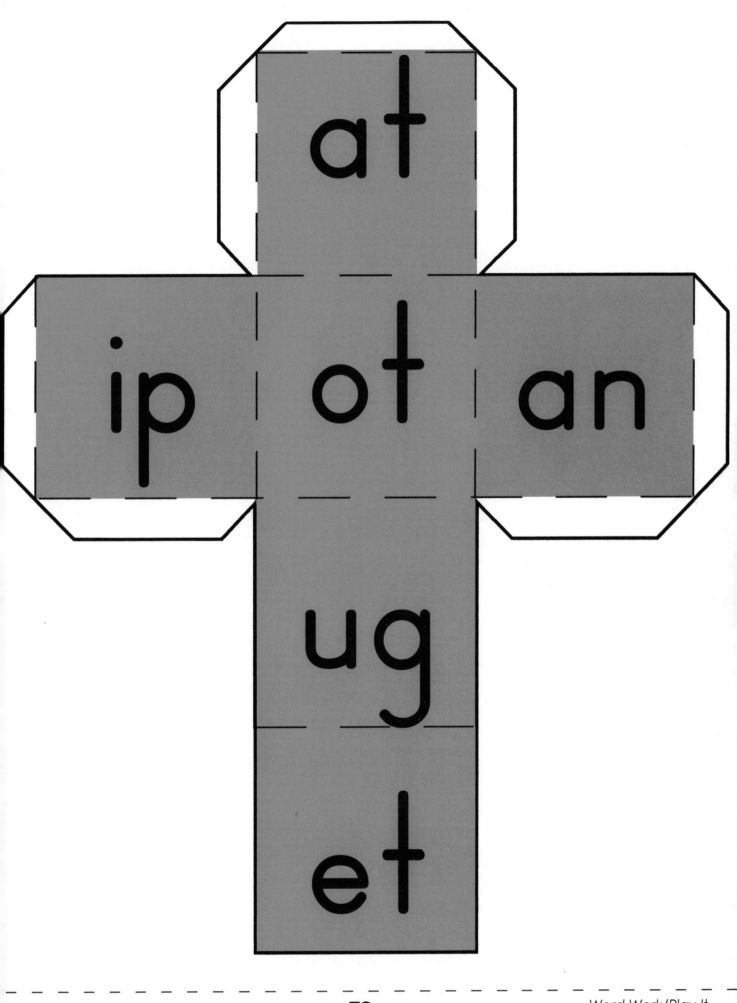

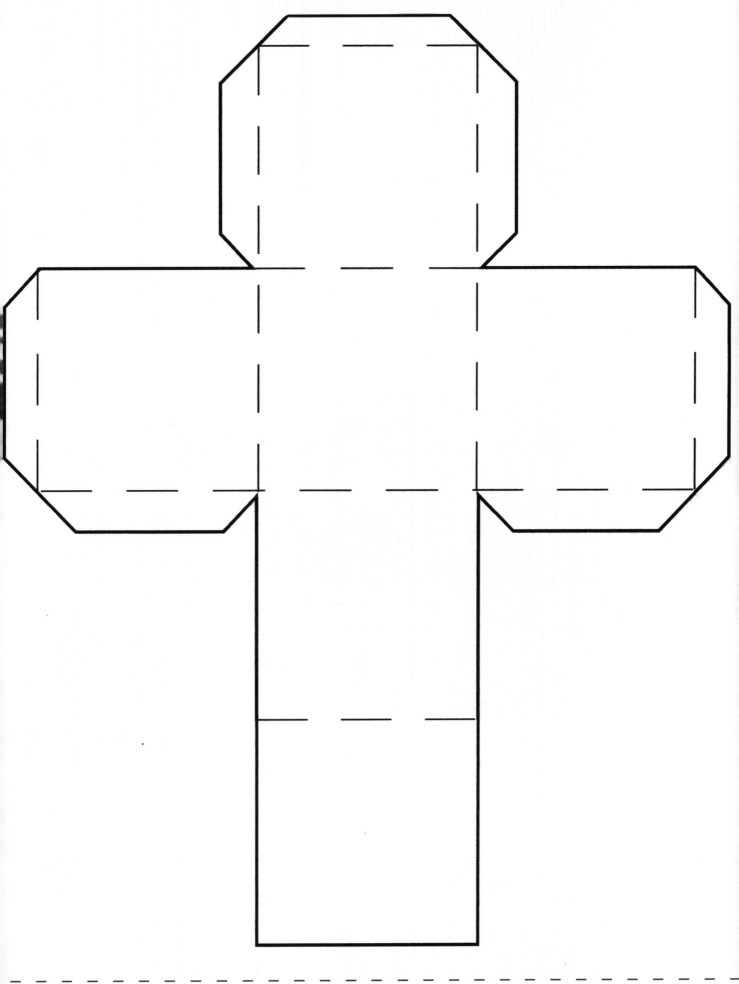

a	a	b	b	c
c	d	d	e	e
f	f	g	g	h
h	i	i	j	j
k	k	l	l	m
m	n	n	o	o

p	p	q	q	r
u	u	v	v	w
r	s	s	t	t
w	x	x	y	y
z	z	z	a	e	i
o	u	a	e	i

85

like	the	went
make	what	blue
see	funny	come
look	play	down
help	three	yellow

Word Work/ Make-a-Word

find	jump	little
said	with	they
there	came	saw
was	are	ran
under	has	well

again	could	every
know	once	over
put	think	where
please	white	this
good	our	from

Word Work/ Make-a-Word

round	walk	why
your	some	goes
does	first	them
new	now	who
open	of	work

been	buy	before
made	call	write
right	pull	their
these	use	which
would	off	about

carry	done	laugh
never	only	start
draw	eight	myself
since	own	when
shall	long	many

together

because

around

always

cat

flap

tan

say

cake

name

let

peg

men

see	green	three
slip	him	thin
kite	ice	find
dot	home	old
rose	rug	club
sun	tube	use

Word Work/ Sorting Sack

name	naym	where	wayr
what	wut	they	thay
with	wiht	funny	funee
said	sed	down	doun
yellow	yelow	has	haz
of	uv	five	fyv

Word Work/ Sorting Sack

black	blac	you	yuw
by	bi	was	wuz

jump	said	come	went
who	like	now	there
when	does	off	would
pretty	away	again	over

before	because	very
many	little	open
however	discover	vacation
beautiful	difficult	exciting
newspaper		together
September		Saturday

Mystery Word

NAME : _____

Use these letters to make words and write them in the boxes below.

Can you figure out the Mystery Word? _____

Name: _____

Squiggle Writing

Write about your squiggle here ↴

 pencil

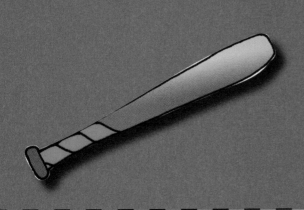 bat

 star

 lunch

frog

cow

king

school

tree

book

house

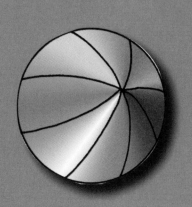

ball

orange

fish

clock

moon

hot	cold	weak	strong
yes	no	young	old
whisper	shout	thick	thin
buy	sell	true	false
difficult	easy	ask	tell
rough	smooth	near	far

smile	grin	thin	skinny
find	locate	easy	simple
allow	permit	part	piece
gift	present	all	whole
sad	unhappy	smart	wise
late	tardy	all	whole

one	1	two	2
three	3	four	4
five	5	six	6
seven	7	eight	8
nine	9	ten	10

twenty	20	thirty	30
forty	40	fifty	50
sixty	60	seventy	70
eighty	80	ninety	90
one hundred		100	
one thousand		1,000	
ten thousand		10,000	
one hundred thousand		100,000	

Name: _____

Character Snapshot

Story Title: _____

Write about the character here. ⤵

_____
_ _ _ _ _ _ _ _ _ _ _ _ _ _ _ _ _ _
_____
_ _ _ _ _ _ _ _ _ _ _ _ _ _ _ _ _ _
_____
_ _ _ _ _ _ _ _ _ _ _ _ _ _ _ _ _ _
_____
_ _ _ _ _ _ _ _ _ _ _ _ _ _ _ _ _ _
_____

_____
_ _
_____
_ _
_____
_ _
_____
_ _
_____

Story Flag

Name: _____

Title: _____

Author: _____

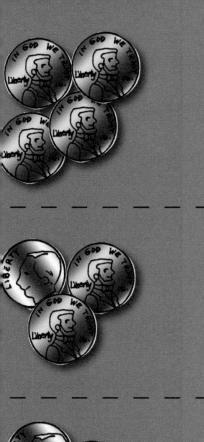 **4¢**

 **7¢**

 **12¢**

 **16¢**

 **21¢**

 **26¢**

 **32¢**

 **40¢**

55¢

 **75¢**

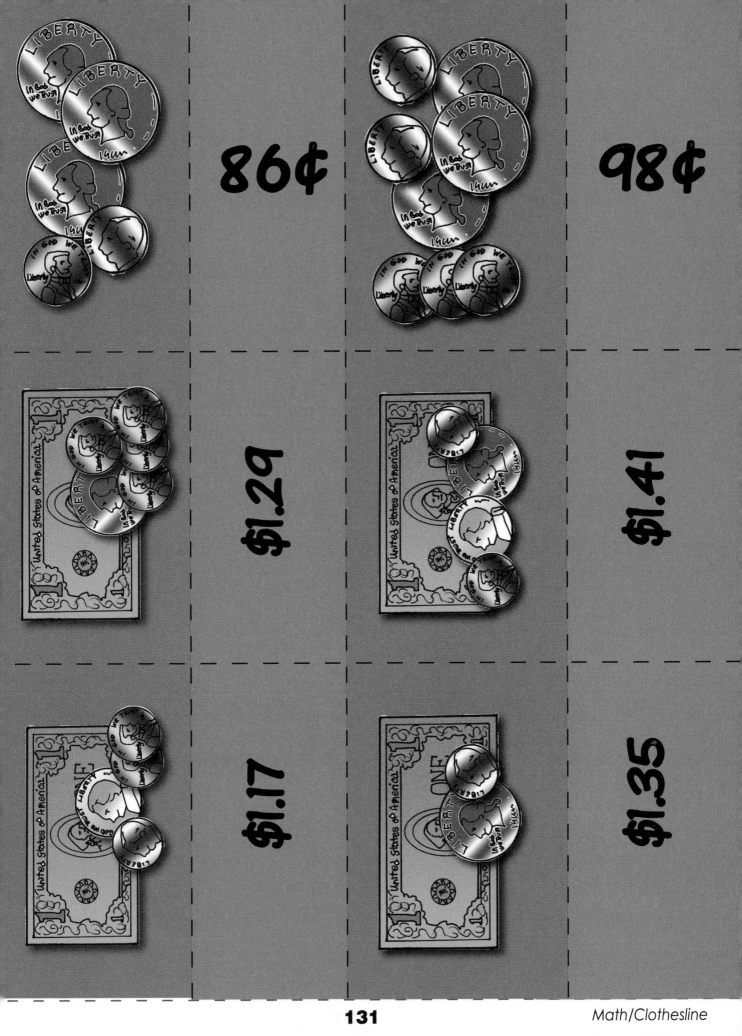

86¢

98¢

$1.29

$1.41

$1.17

$1.35

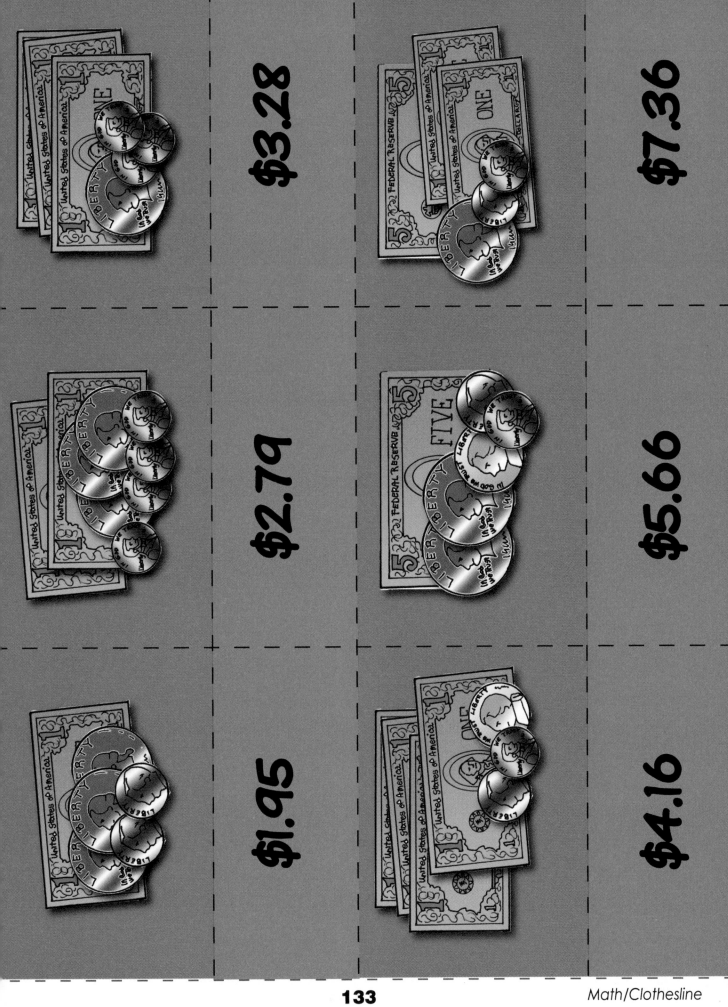

$3.28

$7.36

$2.79

$5.66

$1.95

$4.16

Pocket Change

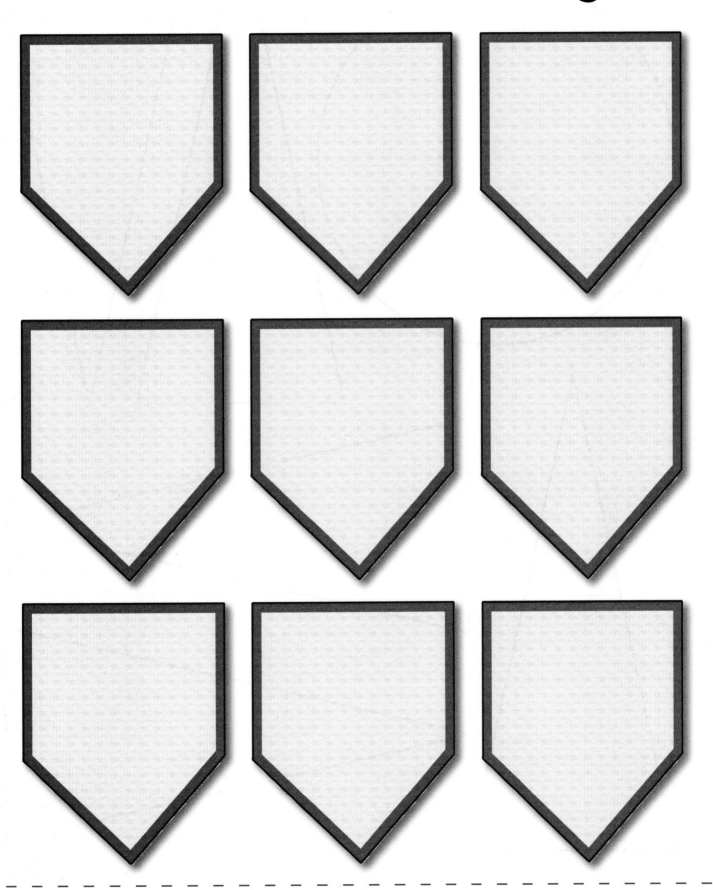

Math/ Pocket Change–Reproducible

Math Suns

137

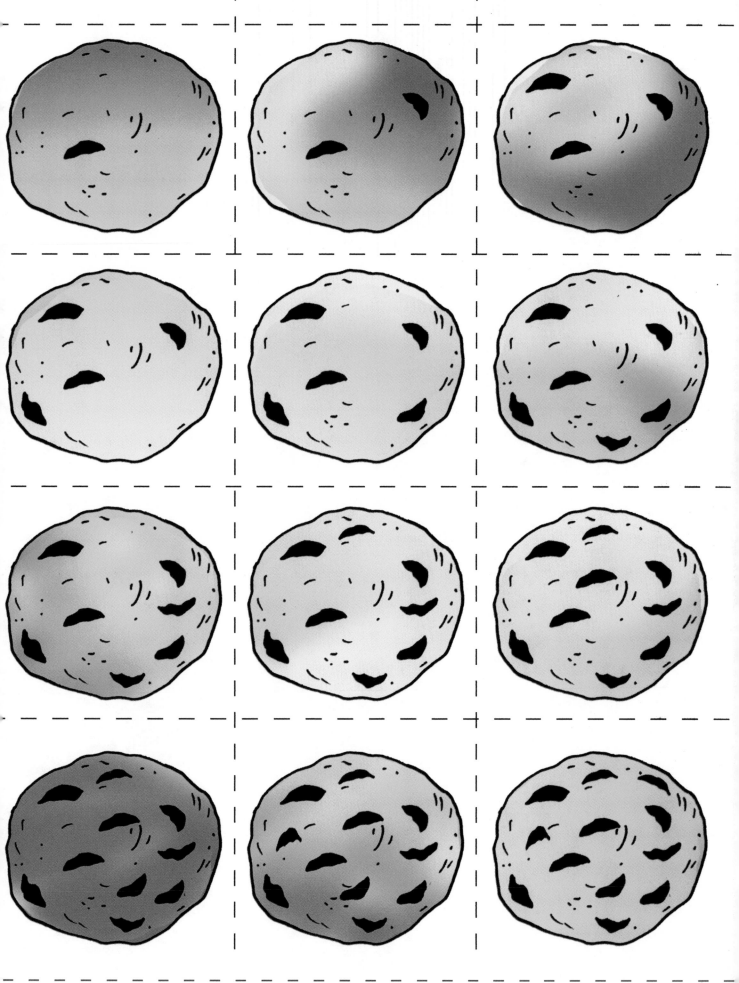

Index

Note: Page numbers in boldface indicate ready-to-use materials and reproducibles.